SPECIAL CEREMONIES

Growing Up

Polly Goodman

WAYLAND

SPECIAL CEREMONIES

Growing Up

This book is based on the original title *Growing Up* by Susan Behar, in the *Ceremonies and Celebrations* series, published in 2000 by Hodder Wayland.

This differentiated text version is by Polly Goodman, published in Great Britain in 2005 by Hodder Wayland, an imprint of Hodder Children's Books.

This paperback edition published in 2006 by Wayland, an imprint of Hachette Children's Books.

Original designer: Tim Mayer
Layout for this edition: Jane Hawkins

Consultants:
Rasamandala Das;
Working Group on Sikhs and Education (WORKSE);
Jane Clements, The Council of Christians and Jews;
Jonathan Gorsky, The Council of Christians and Jews;
Dr Fatma Amer, The London Central Mosque;
The Clear Vision Trust.

Picture acknowledgements:
Hutchison Library 11, 17 (Liba Taylor), 18, 22 (Liba Taylor), 23; Panos Pictures 10 (P Tweedie), 28 John S Paull); Peter Sanders 21; Tony Stone Images 25 (Anthony Cassidy); Trip 1 (G Wittenberg), 4 (I Genut), 5 (Dinodia), 6 (M Fairman), 7 (F Good), 8 (P Joseph), 9 (G Wittenburg), 12 (H Rogers), 19, 20, 24 (Diondia), 26 (A Gasson), 27 (J Batten), 29 (T Bognar).

British Library Cataloguing in Publication Data
Goodman, Polly
Growing up. - Differentiated ed. - (Special Ceremonies)
1. Puberty rites - Juvenile literature 2. Initiation rites - Religious aspects - Juvenile literature
I. Title II. Behar, Susan
203. 8'2

ISBN-10: 0 7502 4973 0
ISBN-13: 978 0 7502 4973 7

Printed in China

Wayland
An imprint of Hachette Children's Books
338 Euston Road, London NW1 3BH

Contents

Becoming an Adult

When they reach a certain age, many children are ready to make a commitment to their religion. They celebrate this in a special ceremony, usually called an initiation ceremony. It marks the time that they become adults and begin to make decisions for themselves.

The age that children have their initiation ceremony varies between different religions, but most ceremonies take place when a child is 12 or 13 years old. At this age, children are old enough to understand the teachings and customs of their faith. They promise to live their lives according to these teachings.

Some religions, such as Islam, do not have separate initiation ceremonies. Muslim babies automatically belong to Islam.

◄ These Jewish boys prepare for their initiation ceremony by reading from the *Torah*, the Jewish holy book.

The ceremony

Most children have special lessons before their initiation ceremony. They learn about their religion's customs and beliefs. Some learn a new language so they can read from their religion's holy book.

Family members help children prepare for their initiation ceremony. ▼

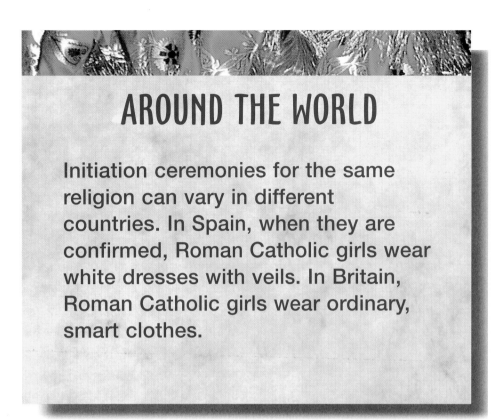

AROUND THE WORLD

Initiation ceremonies for the same religion can vary in different countries. In Spain, when they are confirmed, Roman Catholic girls wear white dresses with veils. In Britain, Roman Catholic girls wear ordinary, smart clothes.

The Christian Tradition

Christian children have two ceremonies where they become members of their faith: baptism and confirmation. Most children are baptized when they are just a few months old. This ceremony is also called a christening, because it is when children are given their Christian names.

Baptisms, or christenings take place in a church. A priest or minister pours holy water over the baby's forehead and welcomes the baby to the Christian faith. The baby's parents choose godparents who promise to help the child grow up as a Christian.

▲ At Sunday school, Christian children read stories or sing songs from the *Bible*, the Christian holy book.

Children learn how to say prayers. They learn about symbols of Christianity, such as the cross. The cross is a Christian symbol because Jesus died on a wooden cross. ▶

Learning about Christianity

Children learn how to be a Christian in different ways. They may go to church on Sundays. Many go to Sunday school, where they read stories about Jesus and learn about his teachings. When they are old enough to understand what being a Christian means, many children confirm their faith. This ceremony is called confirmation.

Most Christian children are confirmed when they are over 13 years old. In the months before their confirmation, children go to special classes. They learn about the ceremony and what it means to be a Christian.

FAYE'S STORY

'My name is Faye. I was confirmed when I was 13. There were 20 other children from my parish getting confirmed at the same time. It was really exciting because we met the bishop in the church. We knelt in front of him and he asked us some questions one by one. I was really nervous when it was my turn to answer.'

◀ At confirmation, Protestant children have their First Communion.

Confirmation

Confirmation ceremonies take place in a church. They are usually led by a bishop. Several children are confirmed at the same time. The bishop asks each child to repeat the promises their parents made for them when they were baptized. They may also be asked questions about their beliefs.

Each child kneels in front of the bishop. He puts his hands on their heads just as Jesus laid his hands on the heads of his disciples. Then the bishop confirms each child in the Christian faith, saying 'Confirm, O Lord, your servant, with your Holy Spirit.' Afterwards, many children take their first Holy Communion.

Holy Communion

At Communion, bread and wine is blessed and given to each person. The bread represents the body of Jesus and the wine represents his blood. Taking Communion reminds Christians about the life and death of Jesus. They remember the last meal that Jesus shared with his disciples, called the Last Supper.

Catholic children have their First Communion when they are 7 years old. Protestant children have their First Communion later, often after their confirmation.

HOLY BOOK

'Let the children come to me... for the Kingdom of God belongs to such as these. I tell you, whoever does not accept the Kingdom of God like a child will never enter it.'

From
The Bible, Mark 10:13

◀ Roman Catholic children in Spain wear white dresses with veils at their confirmation. White is a symbol of purity.

The Jewish Tradition

◄ The *Torah* is written over two scrolls. The boy in this photo is carrying the scrolls to a special table.

Jewish children become adults in the eyes of their religion in a special ceremony. For boys this is called a *bar mitzvah*. It takes place when they are 13 years old. For girls it is called a *bat mitzvah*, and it takes place when they are 12.

In both ceremonies, girls and boys may have to read a section of the *Torah*, the Jewish holy book. It is written in Hebrew, the ancient language of the Jewish people.

No-one is allowed to touch the sacred scrolls of the *Torah* so a special pointer is used to follow the words. The pointer is called a yad. ▶

SARAH'S STORY

'My name is Sarah. My brother David had his *bar mitzvah* last week. He was really nervous because he had to read out loud from the *Torah* in the synagogue. My *bat mitzvah* is next year. I've got to practise reading from the *Torah*, too.'

Learning about Judaism

Jewish girls and boys learn about Judaism from an early age. They go to a special religious school, called a *Cheder*. In the *Cheder*, children learn Hebrew. They are also taught about the Jewish beliefs and practices.

Bar mitzvah

The *bar mitzvah* ceremony takes places during the normal *shabbat* (Saturday) service at the synagogue. For their *bar mitzvah*, boys may wear a prayer shawl called a *tallit*. In the synagogue, the *Torah* is taken out of the place where it is stored, called the *Ark*. It is placed on a reading desk on a platform, called the *bimah*. The boy reads the passage he has learnt from the *Torah* out loud. Afterwards the rabbi, the head of the synagogue, blesses the boy.

Bat mitzvah

In some Jewish communities, the *bat mitzvah* is similar to a *bar mitzvah*. Girls practise reading a section of the *Torah* in Hebrew, and read it out loud in the synagogue. Orthodox Jewish girls celebrate their coming of age in a different way. They read poetry and psalms in a separate party that is not part of a religious service.

After a *bar mitzvah* and *bat mitzvah*, many children have a celebration dinner with family and friends. They thank their parents for their support.

A rabbi (teacher) helps a girl read the *Torah* before her *bat mitzvah* ceremony. ▼

▲ Now this boy has had his *bar mitzvah*, he wears *tefillin* on his forehead and left arm. These are leather boxes with parts of the *Torah* written inside.

Becoming an adult

After their *bar mitzvah* and *bat mitzvah*, boys and girls become adults in the eyes of their religion. They become responsible for their actions and for following the commandments, or Jewish laws. Jews believe God gave these commandments to Moses, a prophet who lived over 3,000 years ago.

HOLY BOOK

'Love the Lord your God with all your heart, and with all your soul and with all your strength. And these words, which I am commanding you today, shall be upon your heart. And you shall teach them carefully to your children.'

From The *Bible: Deuteronomy 6: 4-9*

The Sikh Tradition

◄ This father is tying his son's plaited hair at the back of his head. The father is wearing a turban to keep his uncut hair neat.

When young Sikhs are old enough, they make promises to their religion in a special ceremony, called *Amrit*. Most children are over 14 years old when they take their *Amrit*. They must be old enough to understand the promises they are making and the teachings of the Sikh religion.

The *Amrit* ceremony takes place in the *gurdwara*, the Sikh place of worship. Children read from the *Guru Granth Sahib*, the Sikh holy book. It is written in many languages, including Punjabi, a language from India, so Sikh children have to learn Punjabi.

The *Guru Granth Sahib* teaches about Sikh beliefs. Children also learn about Sikh history and culture from their parents. The family and the Sikh community, called *Khalsa*, are very important to Sikhs.

This photograph shows four of the five 'Ks': *kara* (bracelet), *kirpan* (small sword), *kangha* (comb) and *kachera* (shorts). ▶

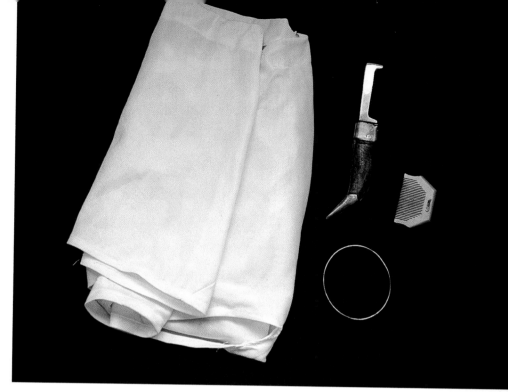

JASDEEP'S STORY

'My name is Jasdeep. I took my *Amrit* last year, when I was 14. I had to learn a prayer from the *Guru Granth Sahib* and read it out loud in the *gurdwara*. I was really nervous, but it was worth it. Now I feel like a real Sikh and part of the family.'

The five Ks

When Sikhs have their *Amrit* ceremony they have to wear five things. These all start with the letter 'K' in Punjabi, so they are called the 'five Ks'. They represent different Sikh beliefs. The five Ks are:

- *kara*: a steel bracelet that stands for the strength of a person's love for God;

- *kirpan*: a small sword, which shows that a person will defend the weak;

- *kesh*: uncut hair, which represents strength;

- *kangha*: a comb, which stands for cleanliness;

- *kachera*: shorts, which symbolize purity.

Uncut hair represents strength to Sikhs, so most Sikh men and women do not cut their hair. Men and some women wear it in a turban, which is a long piece of fabric wound around the head.

This painting shows the tenth guru preparing *amrit*, a bowl of sweet water, for the *Amrit* ceremony. ▶

The *Amrit* ceremony

In the *gurdwara*, several children take their *Amrit* at the same time, all wearing the five Ks. The service is led by five adults, who also wear the five Ks.

The children listen to the responsibilities of being a Sikh and agree to them. After prayers are said, sweet water, called *amrit*, is poured into the childrens' cupped hands for them to drink. This is repeated five times. Then the water is sprinkled over their eyes and into their hair five times.

Afterwards, the children read the first words of the *Guru Granth Sahib*, called the *Mool Mantar*. By reading these words, the children show they are accepting the Sikh religion.

HOLY BOOK

There is one and only one God
Whose name is Truth
God the Creator is without fear, without hate, immortal, without form and is beyond birth and death
And is understood through God's Grace.'

From the *Guru Granth Sahib*:
The Mool Mantar

The *Guru Granth Sahib* contains the words of the people who began Sikhism. Some of it is from people of other religions who agree with the words of Sikhism. ▶

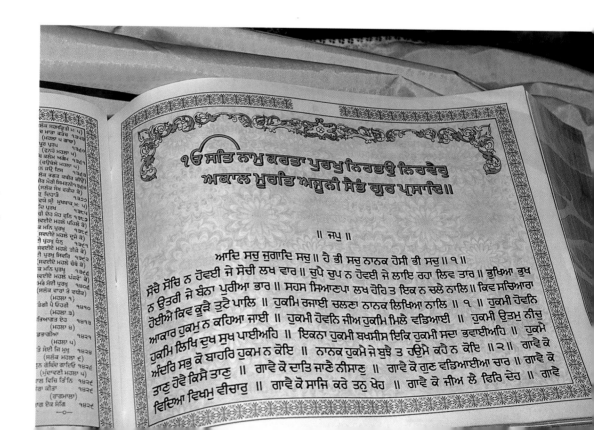

The Muslim Tradition

▲ The *Qur'an* is written in Arabic. It contains the words of Allah, the Muslim word for God.

Muslim children become members of Islam as soon as they are born, so there are no special initiation ceremonies. But children start learning about Islam from an early age. They go to the mosque, the Muslim place of worship, where they learn to pray and read the *Qur'an*, the Muslim holy book.

In India, when children start to learn the *Qur'an*, there is a special ceremony called *Bismallah*. It takes place when a child is 4 years old. Family and friends come to the child's house and the father teaches his child the first lesson from the *Qur'an*. Then everyone eats sweet cakes.

Learning about Islam

Children learn to read the *Qur'an* in special lessons after school or at weekends. Sometimes these classes are at the mosque.

Muslim children are taught to respect themselves and others, and to give to charity. The family is very important to Muslims, and children learn to care for their parents, brothers and sisters.

By the time they are 7 years old, Muslim children must have learnt how to perform the Muslim prayers. These are called *Salah*, and must be performed five times a day. They have also learnt about the Five Pillars of Islam, which are duties for Muslims to follow.

HOLY BOOK

There is no God but Allah. Muhammad ﷺ is the Messenger of Allah.

From *The Pillars of Islam: The First Pillar*

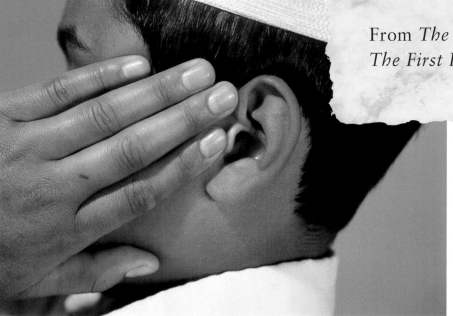

◀ When Muslims start to pray, they raise both hands to their face to help their voices carry further.

The Five Pillars

When they become teenagers, Muslim children are responsible for following the Five Pillars of Islam themselves. These five duties are:

1. Recite the *Shahadah*, or confession of faith.

2. Pray five times a day, known as *Salah*. These prayers are said in Arabic while standing, bowing and kneeling.

3. Give money to charity, called *Zakah*.

4. Fast during *Ramadan*. Muslims fast between sunrise and sunset in the month of *Ramadan* each year.

5. Go on a pilgrimage to Makkah, in Saudi Arabia. This is called *Hajj* and must be done by every Muslim, if they are able to, once in their lifetime.

When they become teenagers, Muslim girls start wearing a headscarf when they go out of their home.

These families are on their pilgrimage, or *Hajj*. ▼

▲ When Muslims pray, they must face towards Makkah, in Saudi Arabia, where Muhammad ﷺ was born.

FATIMAH'S STORY

'My name is Fatimah and I'm ten years old. This year was the first time I've fasted at *Ramadan*. I got up before sunrise and ate breakfast, but between dawn and sunset I didn't eat anything. I drank a lot of water, but that's allowed. At the end of the day, I broke the fast by eating a big meal with my family.'

The *Qur'an*

The *Qur'an* is the Muslim holy book. Muslims believe it contains the words that Allah (God) said to Muhammad ﷺ, the last prophet and final messenger from God. The words give Muslims guidance on Islamic beliefs, laws and customs, and how to live their lives. All around the world, whatever their language, Muslims learn to recite the *Qur'an* in Arabic.

The Hindu Tradition

Hindus believe there are sixteen steps in a person's life, and each step should be celebrated with a special ritual. The rituals are called *samskaras*. The first three *samskaras* take place before a child is born. The next six take place in the child's first few years.

The tenth step is usually for boys between the ages of 7 and 14. It is celebrated by the sacred thread ceremony, or *Upanayana*. This is when a boy becomes a full member of his community. He is old enough to understand the meaning of belonging to the Hindu community and is twice-born into the Hindu religion.

This boy is putting on his sacred thread. ▼

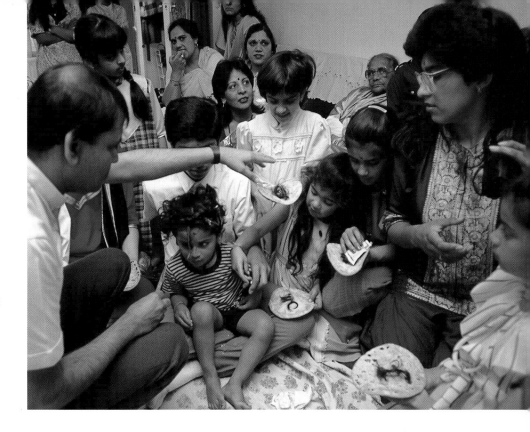

A young Hindu boy may have his hair cut as part of an initiation ceremony. ▶

The *Vedas*

The *Vedas* are part of the Hindu holy scriptures. They are written in Sanskrit, an ancient Indian language. Some Hindu children start to learn Sanskrit when they are about 5 years old. By the time of their sacred thread ceremony, Hindu boys are able to read and begin study of the *Vedas*.

The *Vedas* were written over 3,000 years ago. They contain hymns, stories and poems about God. At a boy's sacred thread ceremony, he will be taught a verse from the first scripture of the *Vedas*.

VIRAN'S STORY

'My name is Viran. For my sacred thread ceremony I had my hair cut and put on white cotton clothes. White stands for cleanliness and my second birth into the Hindu religion. After the ceremony we had a big dinner with my family to celebrate.'

The ceremony

The sacred thread ceremony usually takes place in a boy's home, in front of family, friends and Hindu priests. Before the ceremony, the boy may have his hair cut or his head completely shaved. He wears simple cotton clothing to symbolize cleanliness and rebirth.

A priest gives the boy a loop of cotton thread made from three strands. The boy wears the sacred thread over his left shoulder, across his chest and under his right arm. He is given a staff (stick) to hold and grass string is tied around his waist.

▲ A boy holds a staff across his right shoulder in his sacred thread ceremony, dressed in a simple cotton robe.

SACRED TEXT ॐ

We meditate on the glory and brilliance of the Sun God who lights up the heavens and the Earth. May he bless us and inspire us.

From *Rig Veda: Gayatri mantra*

The boy is taught how to read out a verse from the *Vedas*. He makes a promise to carry out his duties towards God, his parents and his elders.

After the ceremony, the boy is given presents and there is usually a big meal to celebrate with family and friends.

◄ Young Hindu boys may wear yellow turbans at their sacred thread ceremony because yellow is a lucky colour.

The Buddhist Tradition

In Buddhism, there are no special ceremonies to mark the time that children join the Buddhist religion or become adults. But parents may teach their children how to meditate, and live kindly and wisely.

Buddhism was founded by an Indian prince who was born over 2,500 years ago. He became known as the Buddha. The Buddha taught that people can become perfectly wise and kind, if they lead their lives according to his teachings. These are called *Dharma*.

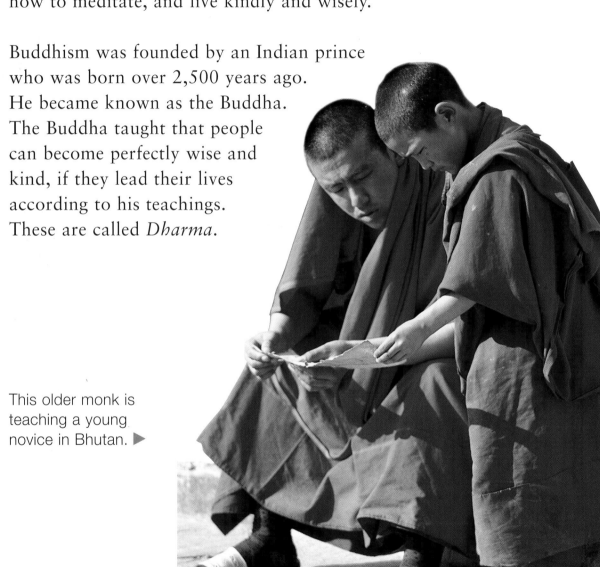

This older monk is teaching a young novice in Bhutan. ▶

This young novice monk is reading from the Buddhist scriptures. ▶

Monks and nuns

Some children join Buddhist monasteries or nunneries to learn about Buddhism. Young monks and nuns are called novices.

When novices join a monastery or nunnery, they shave their heads and put on a simple robe. This reminds them that the Buddha gave up the riches he had as a prince, to become a holy man.

In the monastery or nunnery, the novices learn about Buddhism as well as other subjects such as geography and maths. They spend time meditating and chanting with the monks and nuns, and help them with tasks such as cleaning and cooking.

Like all other Buddhists, they put their trust in The Three Jewels; the Buddha, his teachings (*Dharma*) and the monastery (*Sangha*).

NAGAMUDRA'S STORY

'My name is Nagamudra. I stayed in a monastery last year for four months. I learnt how to meditate and pray. After dinner every night I helped the monks wash the dishes. I missed my family quite a lot but the monks were very kind and I made lots of friends.'

Meditation

Meditation is very important to Buddhists and some children learn to meditate from an early age. Buddhists believe that meditation helps them to become calmer and wiser. They meditate by sitting on the floor with their eyes closed. They stay quiet and still as their minds and bodies feel more and more peaceful.

Many Buddhists meditate for a short time every day. Monks and nuns sometimes meditate for many hours at a time.

Meditation is just one of eight ways of life the Buddha taught.

When Buddhists meditate, they clear their mind of everyday thoughts. ▼

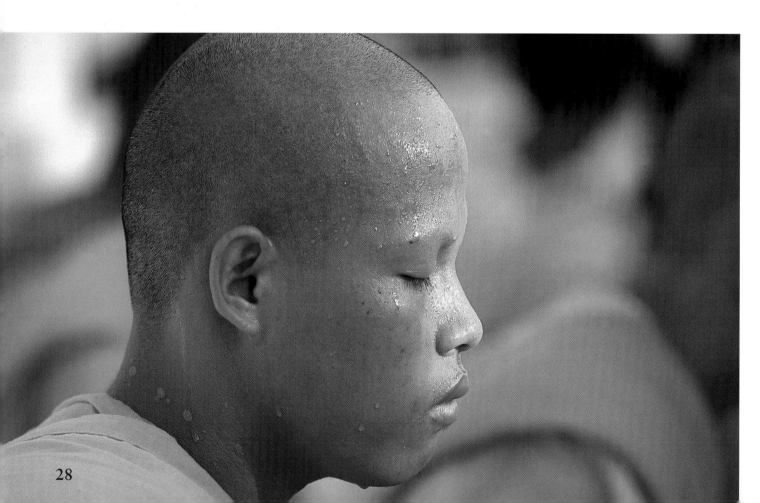

◄ This girl has shaved her head as a sign of the fresh start she is making to become a nun.

SACRED WRITINGS

I go to the Buddha for refuge
I go to the Dharma for refuge
I go to the Sangha for refuge.

From the *Pali Canon:*
The Three Refuges

A Buddhist life

Apart from meditation, the Buddha taught other ways that people should lead their lives. Young Buddhists are taught these things. They learn to try to:

1. Understand what the Buddha said about life.

2. Develop a strong wish to follow his teachings.

3. Speak kindly and truthfully.

4. Be kind and thoughtful in everything they do.

5. Choose a job that does not hurt people, animals or the environment.

6. Avoid both laziness and trying too hard.

7. Be aware of their thoughts and feelings.

8. Meditate regularly.

Glossary

Allah the Muslim word for God.

amrit a mixture of sugar and water used in Sikh ceremonies.

Amrit the ceremony that marks a young Sikh's entry into the Sikh community.

Bible the Christian and Jewish scriptures.

Buddha an Indian prince called Siddhartha Gautama who founded Buddhism.

faith another word for religion, or a belief in a religion.

gurdwara a Sikh place of worship.

guru a Sikh leader.

Guru Granth Sahib the Sikh holy book.

Makkah a city in Saudi Arabia that is holy to Muslims because the Prophet Muhammad ﷺ was born there.

meditate to focus the mind on one thing to achieve wisdom and calm.

monastery a place where monks live and worship.

mosque a Muslim place of worship.

prophet a person who tells what will happen in the future.

Punjabi a language that started in the Punjab, an area that is split between India and Pakistan.

Qur'an the Muslim holy book.

rabbi a teacher of the Jewish religion and head of a synagogue, the Jewish place of worship.

Ramadan the Muslim month of fasting.

Sangha the Buddhist community.

Sanskrit an ancient Indian language used in the Buddhist and Hindu scriptures.

scriptures holy writings.

symbolize to represent something.

synagogue a Jewish place of worship.

Torah the Jewish holy writings, written over two scrolls.

Upanayana the sacred thread ceremony, a Hindu ceremony that marks the beginning of a boy's religious education.

Books to Read

Beliefs and Cultures series: *Buddhist; Christian; Hindu; Jewish; Muslim* (Watts, 2003)

My Life, My Religion series: *Anglican Curate; Catholic Priest; Hindu Priest; Jewish Rabbi; Muslim Imam; Sikh Granthi* (Watts, 2001)

Our Culture series: *Buddhist; Hindu; Jewish; Muslim; Sikh* (Watts, 2003)

Places of Worship series: *Buddhist Temples; Catholic Churches; Hindu Temples; Mosques; Protestant Churches; Sikh Gurdwaras; Synagogues* (Heinemann, 2000)

Rites of Passage: Coming of Age by Mandy Ross (Heinemann, 2003)

A World of Festivals: Life and Death by Jean Coppendale (Chrysalis, 2005)

A Year of Religious Festivals series: *My Buddhist Year; My Christian Year; My Hindu Year; My Jewish Year; My Muslim Year; My Sikh Year* (Hodder Wayland, 2004/2005)

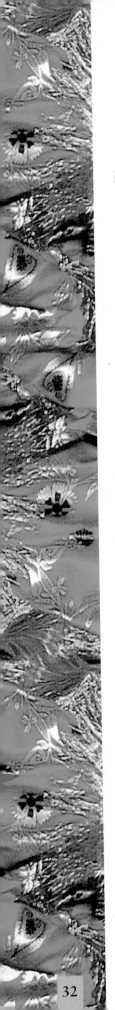

Index

All the numbers in **bold** refer to photographs